PLANTAS
PLANTS

This book provides bilingual materials to teach a fun and comprehensive unit about PLANTS. Included is a teacher's instruction section with details for each project along with ideas to use throughout the classroom. Discover PLANTS using skills in reading, math, and spelling. Both Spanish and English versions of each project are included in one book!

Cover Photos:
© 2002 Brand X Photos
© Photodisc

ISBN 1-59441-641-9

Dear Family Letter (pages 6–7)

Dear Family,

We are starting a unit about PLANTS. We will learn about plants and plant parts.

Please join us by including daily conversations about plants at home. Family discussions will help reinforce the concepts we are learning in class.

When visiting the public library, look for books about plants with your child.

Thank you for helping your child learn more about plants!

Sincerely,

Send this note home with students to let families know what is happening in the classroom. The letter introduces families to the upcoming unit about plants.

Plants Certificates (pages 8–9)

This is a great way to recognize and reward students as they progress through this unit about PLANTS.

Use the Plants Certificates as incentives when students finish a defined list of projects or as general awards when the unit is complete. The certificates make a great classroom bulletin board display and provide students with take-home diplomas that they can be proud of.

Copy the certificates onto colorful paper or let students color their own certificates as a classroom art project.

Plant Cards (pages 10–12)

The plant cards included in this book can be used in a variety of creative ways to make learning with flash cards fun and interesting.

Flash Cards
Make different flash card decks of varying degrees of difficulty to use as assessment tools. Display transparencies of the cards for reference during classroom discussions.

Assembly Instructions
Copy the desired word cards onto colorful, sturdy paper and cut them out. Copy the English cards on one side and the Spanish cards on the other side. Or, copy the picture cards on one side and the English or Spanish word cards on the other side. Laminate cards for permanent use in the classroom or make sets for each student to use at home.

Concentration
This ever-popular game helps students develop memory and matching skills. Concentration works best when played in small groups.

There are several variations of "Plant Concentration." Increase difficulty by mixing and matching combinations. For example, students can match plant picture cards to plant word cards.

Assembly Instructions
Copy the desired plant cards onto sturdy paper and cut them out. Laminate cards for permanent use.

How to Play
1. Mix up the cards and place them facedown in rows.
2. Have students take turns choosing two cards at a time. If a student chooses two cards that match, she takes another turn. If there is no match, she turns the cards facedown, and the next player takes a turn. The player with the most matched pairs wins the game!

Bulletin Board Strips (pages 13–15)

Create bulletin boards for specific parts of plants or themes, such as "My Favorite Plants" or "Things I Know About Plants." Enlarge the strips to make plant bulletin board borders. Then, have students color the pictures on the strips.

Plant Mobiles (pages 16–19)

This fun art project reinforces the skills and vocabulary learned in the PLANTS unit. Use it as a classroom decoration or to identify centers that focus on specific parts of plants.

Assembly Instructions

Select a header card and the desired plant cards for a mobile and copy onto sturdy paper. Use the picture or word plant cards (pages 10–12) or use the mobile cards that include the names and pictures of the plant parts (pages 18–19). Provide crayons, paint, or markers and have students color their mobile pieces. After coloring, have students fold the header cards and punch holes as indicated. Let them tape string, yarn, fishing line, or dental floss to the backs of the word cards. Then, have them glue the coordinating picture card to the back of each word card. When the glue has dried, let them tie the plant cards to the header cards. Hang the mobiles from the ceiling or in a window.

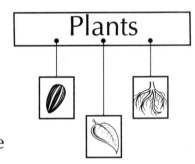

Sentence Strips (pages 20–25)

The sentence strips reinforce basic concepts presented throughout the unit about plants. The strips may be used in bulletin board displays, centers, pocket charts, and as examples for story-starter books.

Roots get minerals and	water from the ground	to help feed plants.

My Plant Books (pages 26–35)

Students can create and color their own books about plants. Teachers can design the books to complement a theme by choosing various pages.

Assembly Instructions

Copy one book for each student. Copy cover pages onto sturdy paper and copy inside pages onto 8½" x 11" (21.5 cm x 28 cm) white paper. Fold, assemble, and bind books using brass fasteners or staples.

Students can write stories or facts about different plants or plant parts in their books. Have students share their finished books with the class.

These books make a great take-home project. Have students complete several books to create their own "My Plants" libraries! Completed books also make an excellent bulletin board display.

My Plant Number Book
(pages 36–43)

This book is a fun and interesting way to integrate plants and counting! Have students color and assemble their own books or copy each page onto colorful paper and laminate for permanent use.

Estimada familia,

Estamos comenzando una unidad sobre las plantas. Aprenderemos acerca de las plantas y las partes de la planta.

Por favor únanse a nosotros e incluyan conversaciones en casa acerca de las plantas, a diario. Las conversaciones familiares ayudan a reforzar los conceptos que se estudian en clase.

Cuando visiten la biblioteca pública, ayuden a sus hijos a buscar libros informativos acerca de las plantas.

Gracias por ayudar a sus hijos a aprender sobre las plantas.

Atentamente,

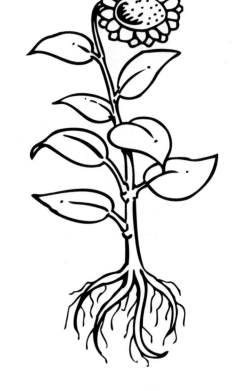

Dear Family,

We are starting a unit about PLANTS. We will learn about plants and plant parts.

Please join us by including daily conversations about plants at home. Family discussions will help reinforce the concepts we are learning in class.

When visiting the public library, look for books about plants with your child.

Thank you for helping your child learn more about plants!

Sincerely,

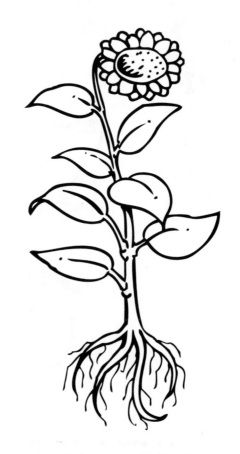

PLANTAS

CERTIFICADO

¡Yo conozco las plantas!

Nombre: _____

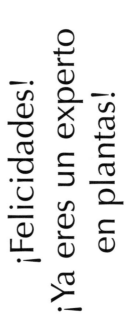

¡Felicidades!
¡Ya eres un experto en plantas!

PLANTS

CERTIFICATE

I know about PLANTS!

Name: _____

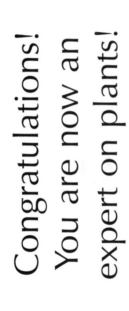

Congratulations!
You are now an
expert on plants!

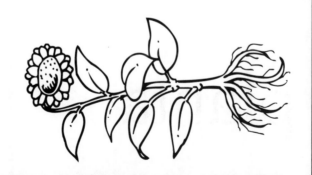

hoja	flor
tallo	semilla
planta	sistema de raíces

flower	leaf
seed	stem
root system	plant

12

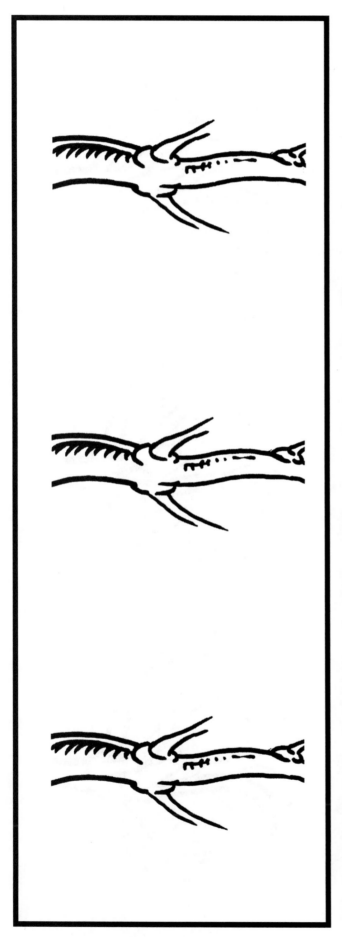

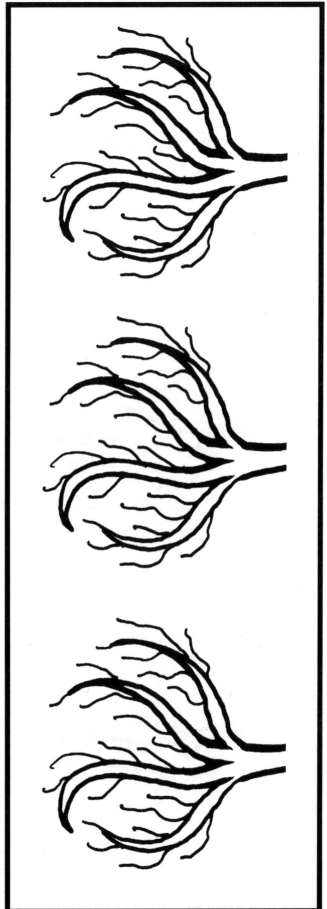

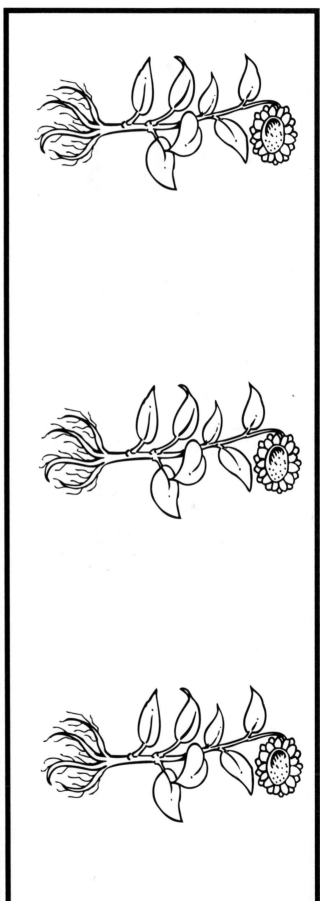

Móviles de las plantas

Plantas

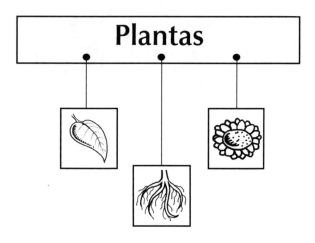

Plantas

Plantas

Plant Mobiles

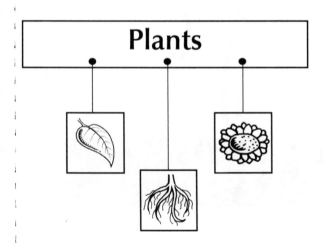

Plants

Plants

Plants

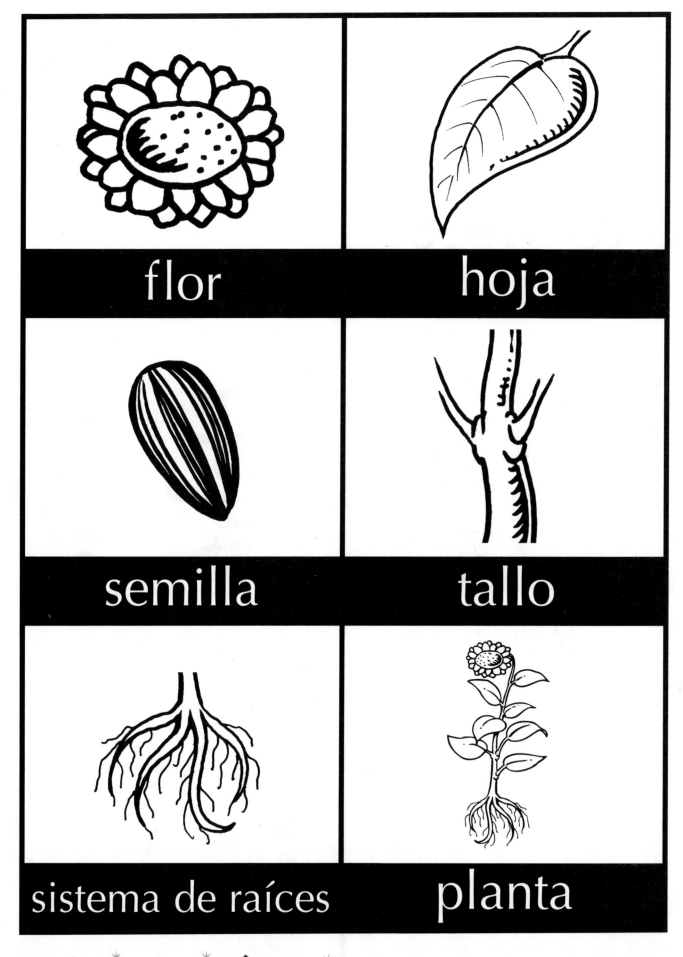

flor

hoja

semilla

tallo

sistema de raíces

planta

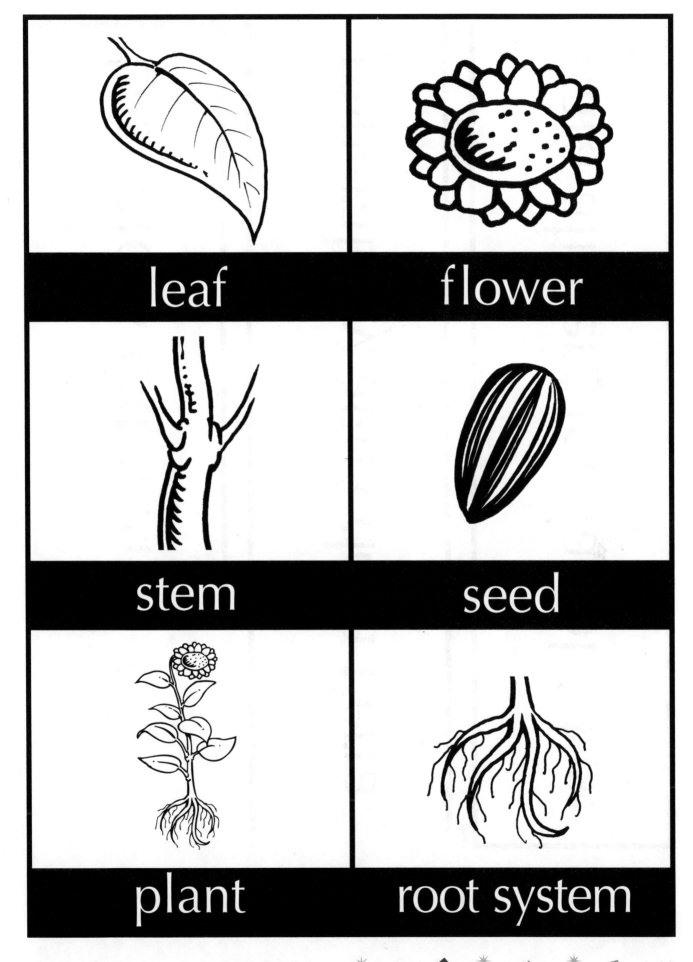

leaf

flower

stem

seed

plant

root system

Las raíces extraen

minerales y agua de la tierra

para alimentar a las plantas.

Roots get minerals and

water from the ground

to help feed plants.

Los tallos llevan agua y

minerales desde las raíces

hasta las hojas de las plantas.

Stems carry water and minerals to the leaves from the roots.

Una semilla contiene

el principio de la vida

de una planta nueva.

A seed contains the

beginnings of a new plant.

Conozco las plantas

Este libro fue
hecho por:

Nombre: _____

I Know About Plants

This Book Was
Created By:

Name: _____

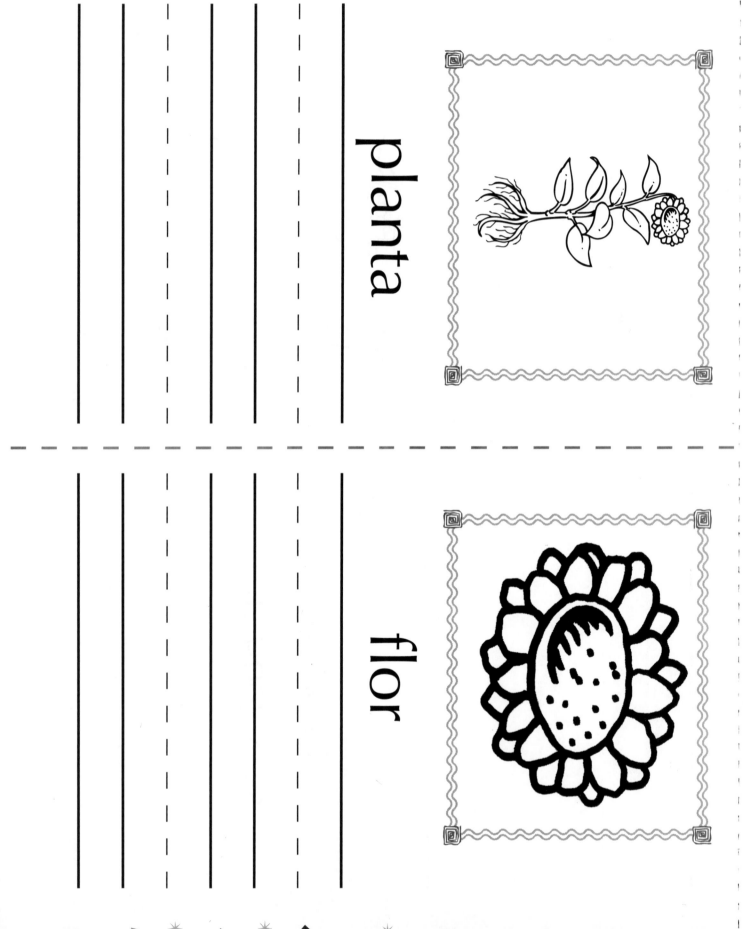

planta

flor

plant

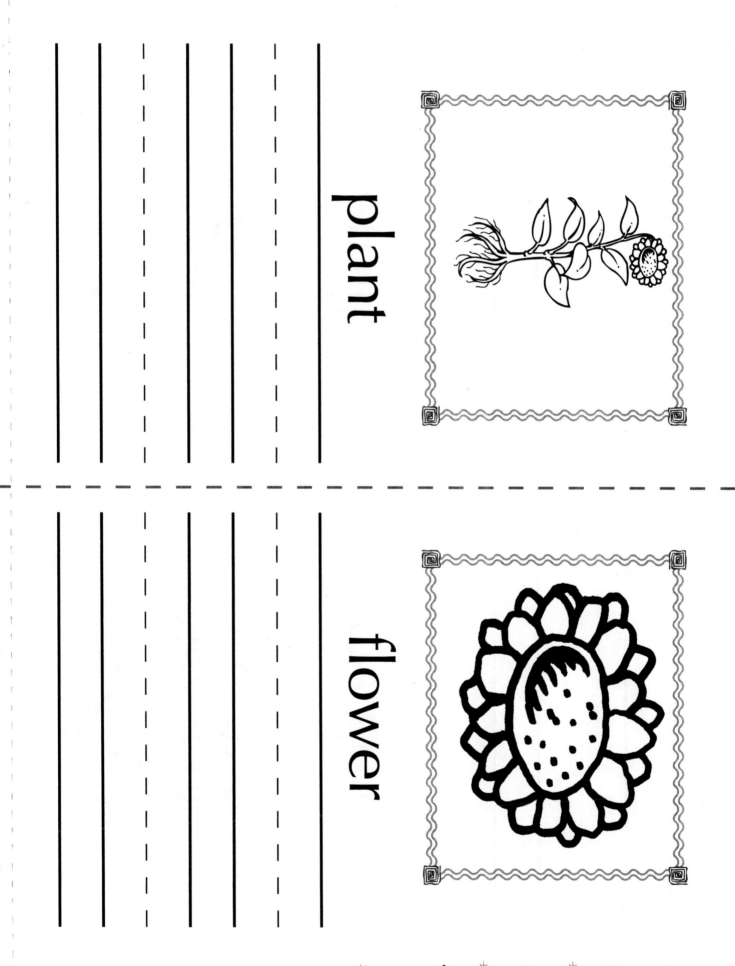

flower

semilla

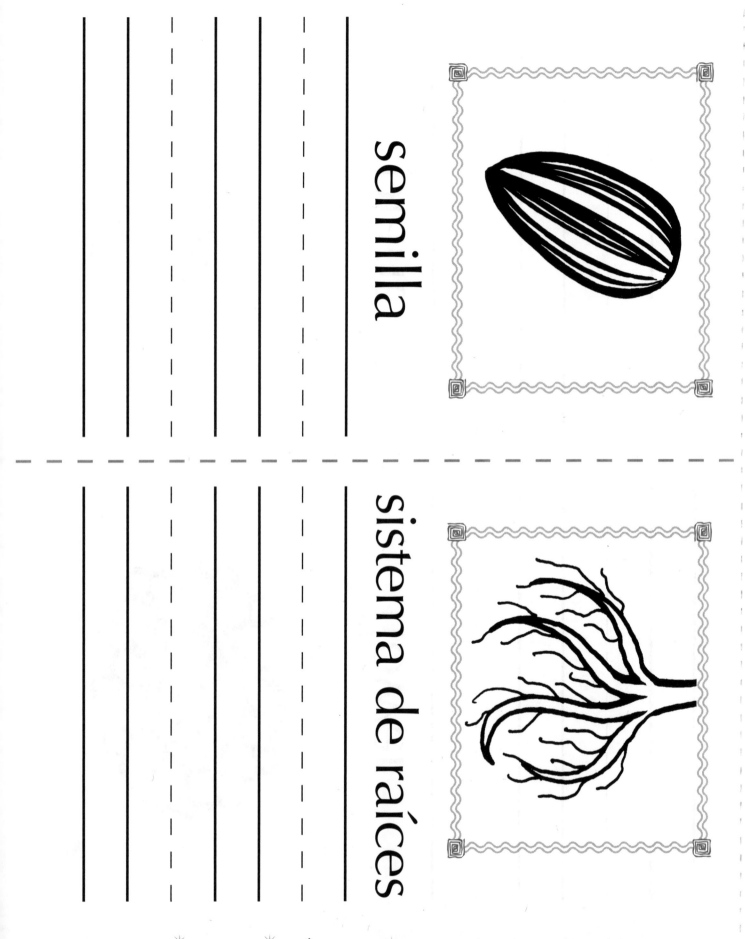

sistema de raíces

seed

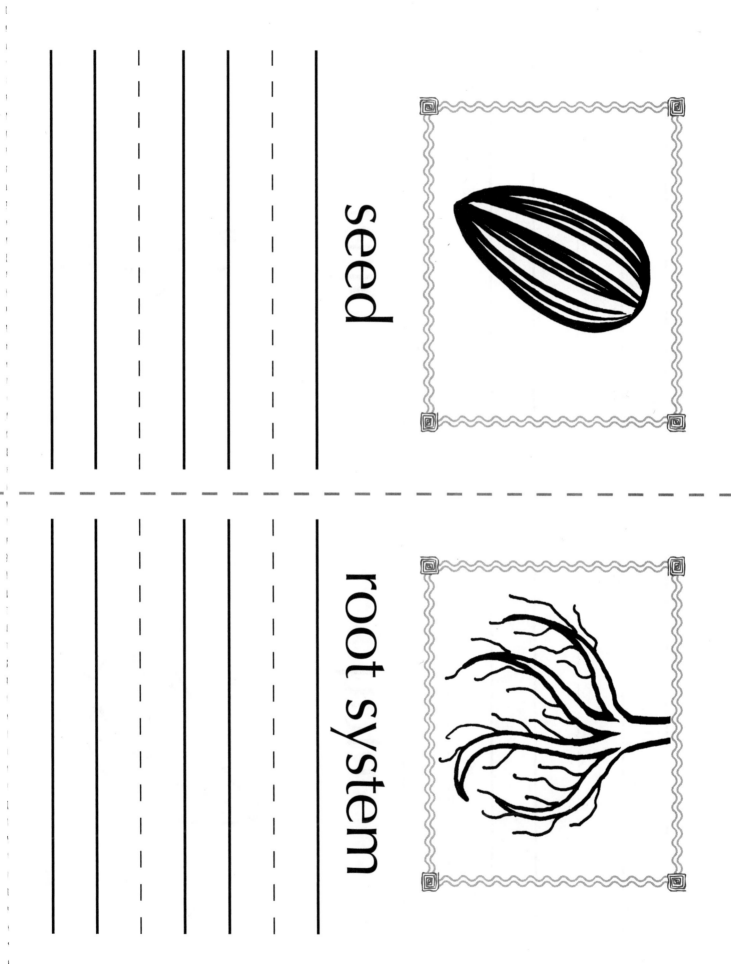

root system

tallo

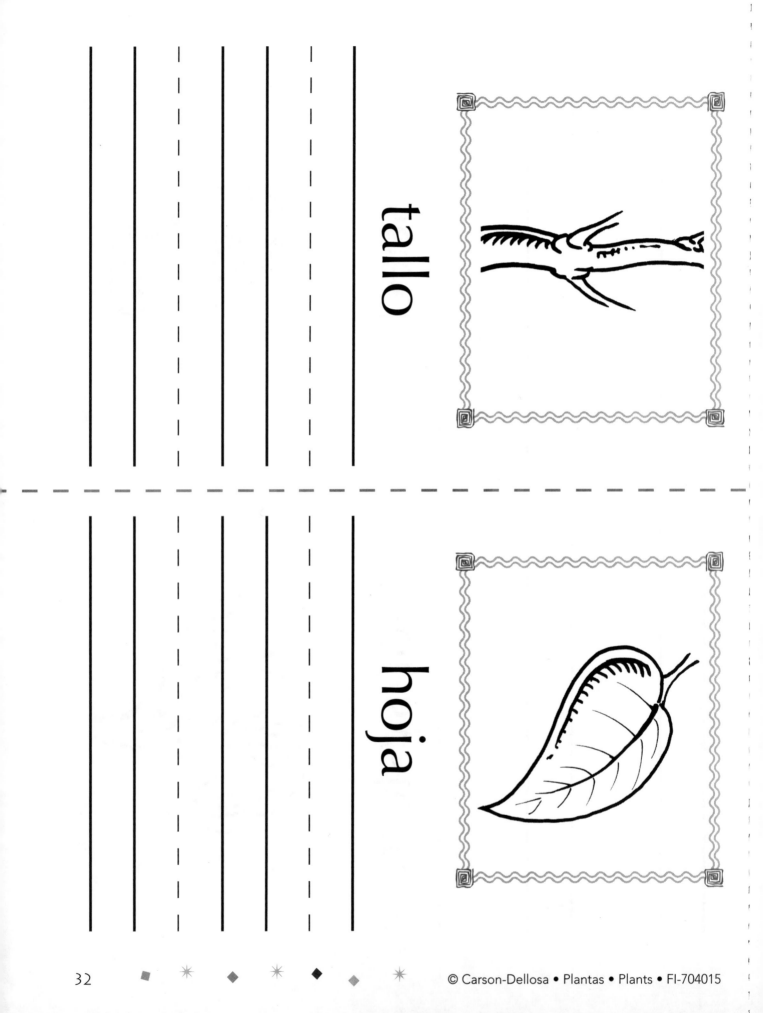

hoja

stem

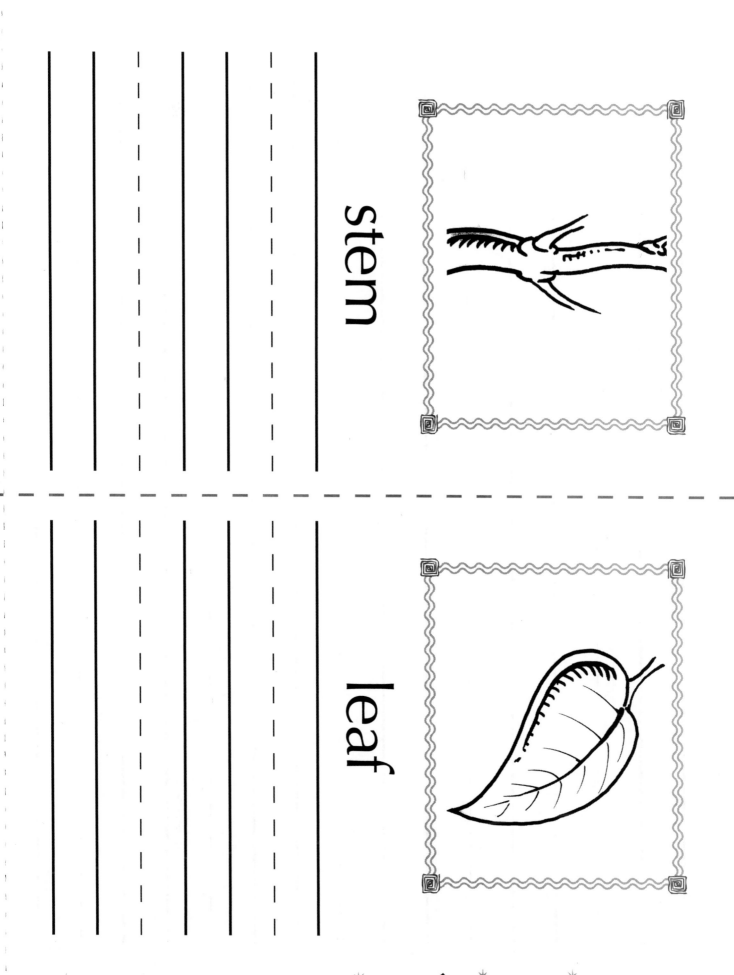

leaf

34

Mi libro de
los números
sobre las
plantas

Por _____

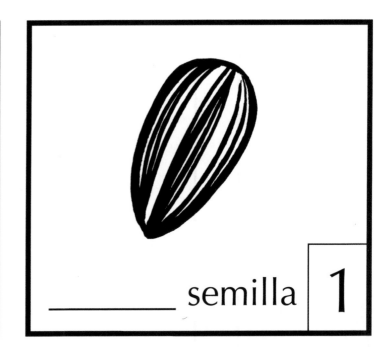

_____ semilla | 1

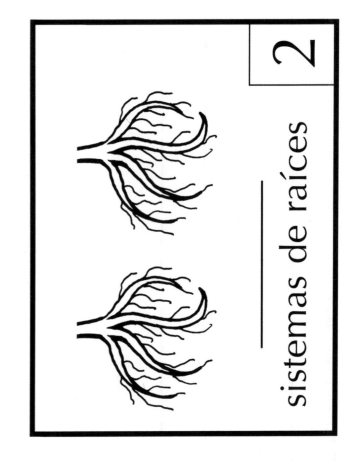

_____ tallos | 3

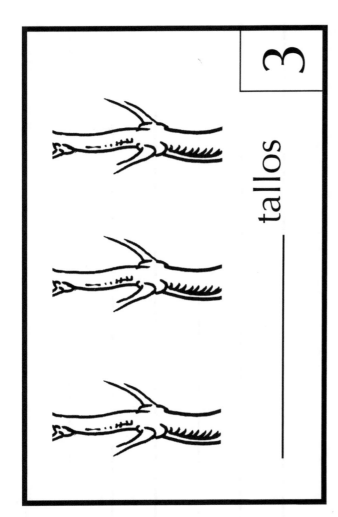

sistemas de raíces | 2

My
Plant
Number
Book

by _____

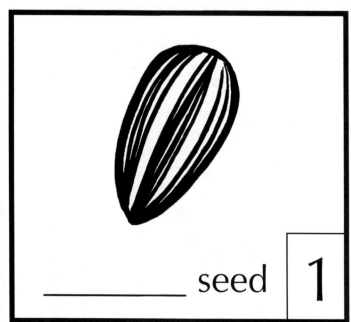

_____ seed

1

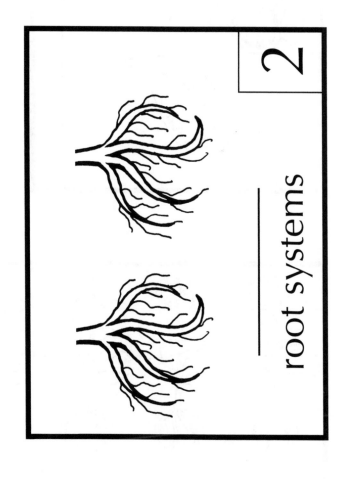

stems

3

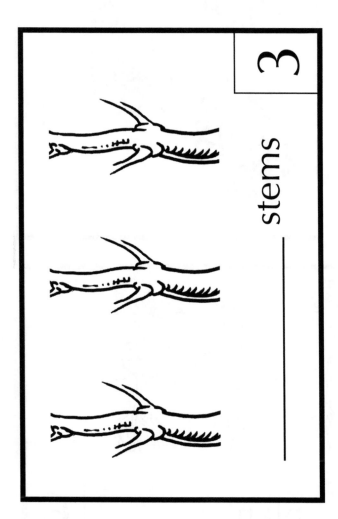

root systems

2

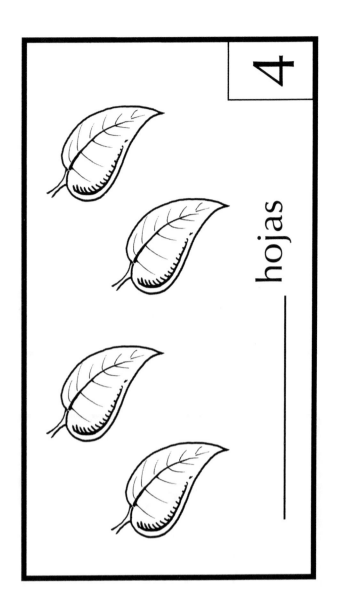

4

_____ hojas

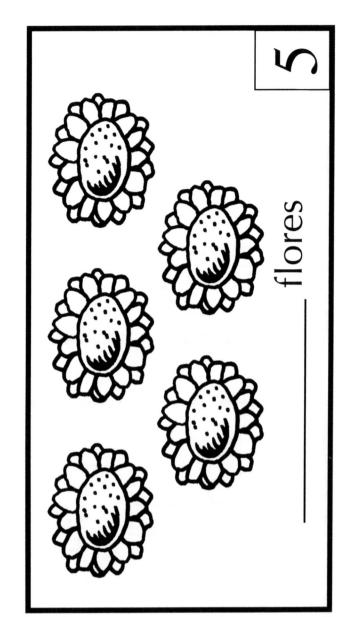

5

_____ flores

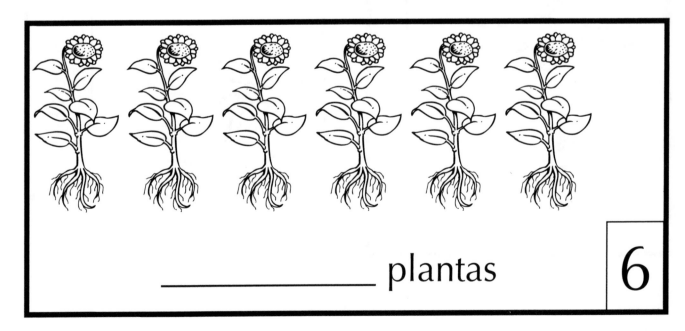

_____ plantas

6

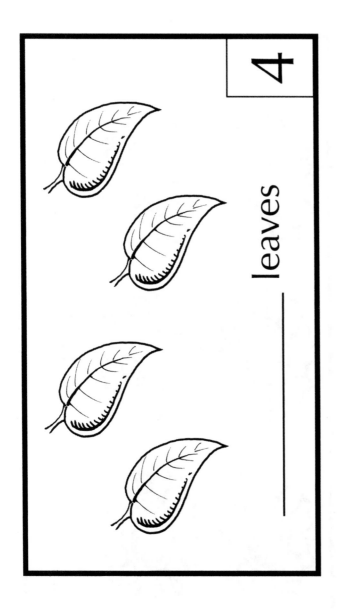

4

_____ leaves

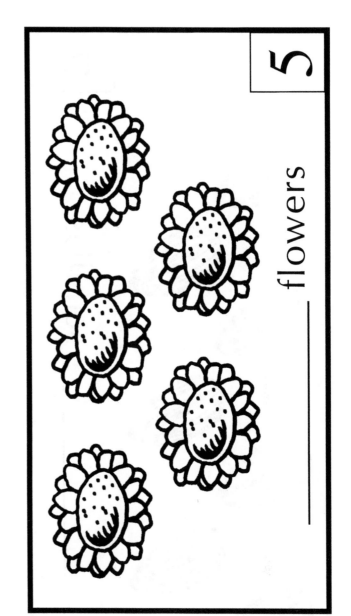

5

_____ flowers

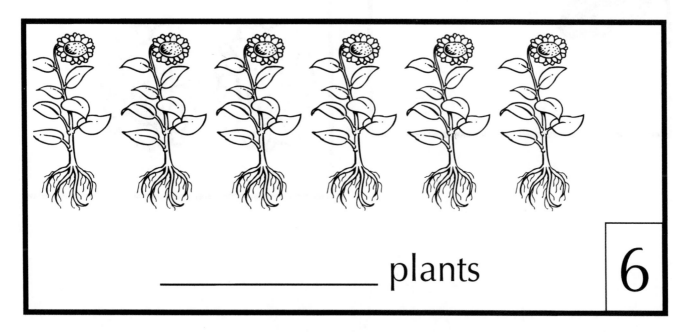

_____ plants

6

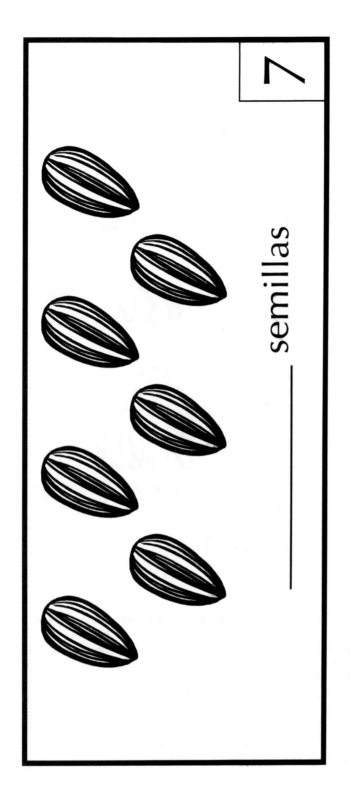

7

semillas

_____

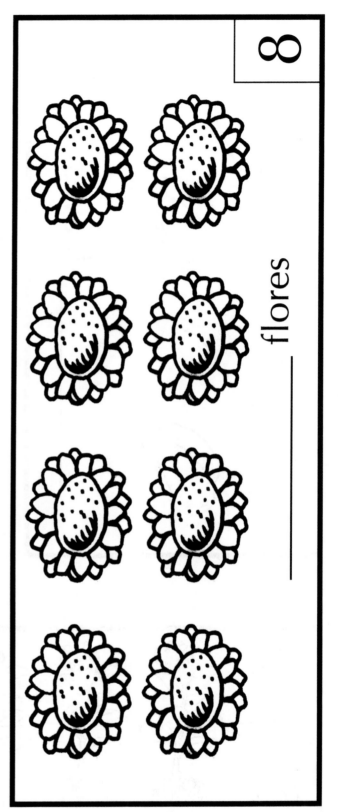

8

flores

_____

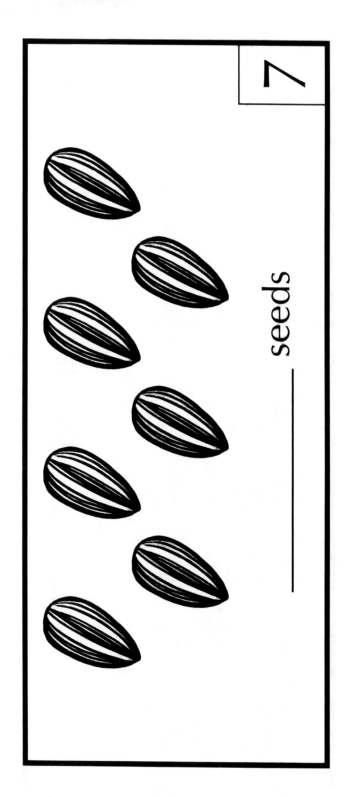

7

seeds ___

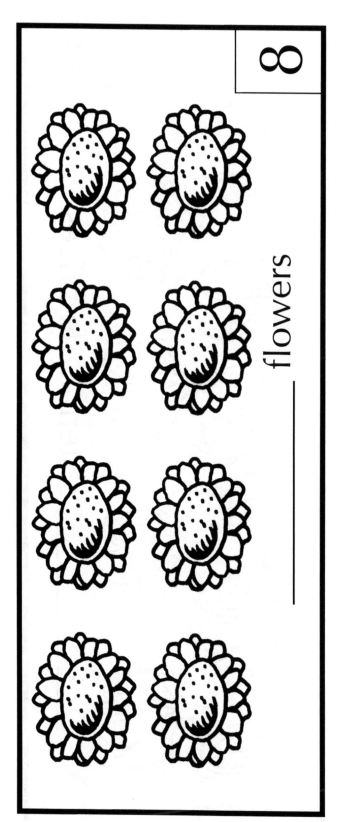

8

flowers ___

9

sistemas de raíces

10

plantas

9

root systems

_____

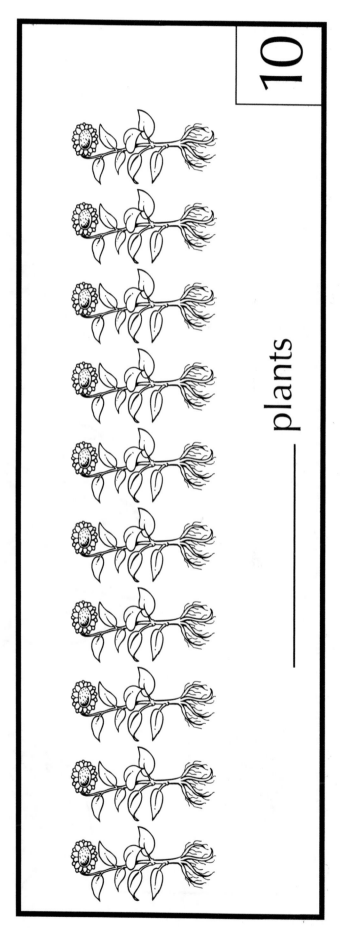

10

plants

_____

Nombre: _____

Partes de la planta

Escribe el nombre de cada parte de la planta en su línea correspondiente.

1. _____

2. _____

3. _____

4. _____

5. _____

Name: _____

 **Plant Parts** Write the name of each plant part on the correct line.

1. _____

2. _____

3. _____

4. _____

5. _____

Nombre: _____

 Nombres de las partes de la planta

Traza una línea desde el nombre hasta el dibujo correcto.

hoja

semilla

flor

tallo

planta

sistema de raíces

Name: _____

 **Plant Part Match**

leaf

seed

flower

stem

plant

root system

Nombre: _____

 Haz un círculo alrededor de las hojas.

¿Cuántos círculos hiciste? _____

Name: _____

 Circle all of the leaves.

How many leaves did you circle? _____

Nombre: _____

Haz un círculo alrededor de las semillas.

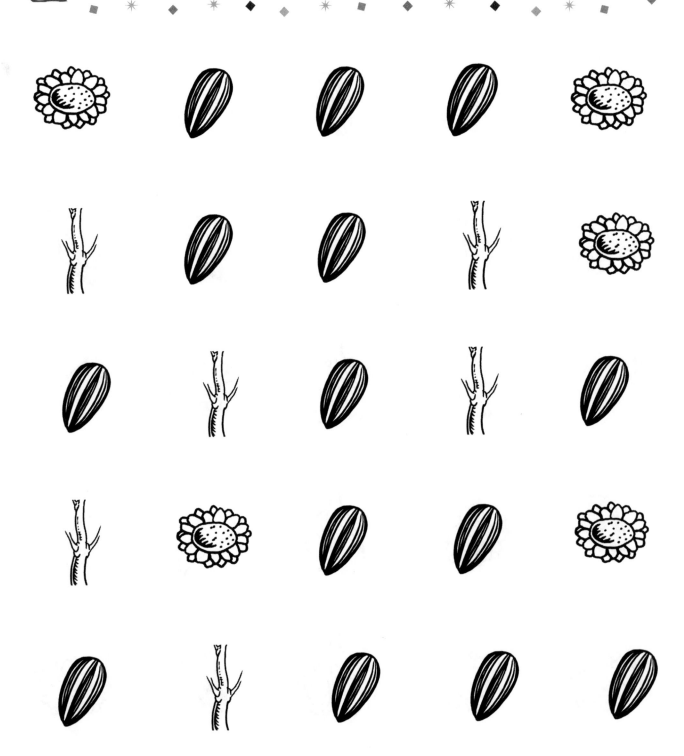

¿Cuántos círculos hiciste? _____

Name: _____

 Circle all of the seeds.

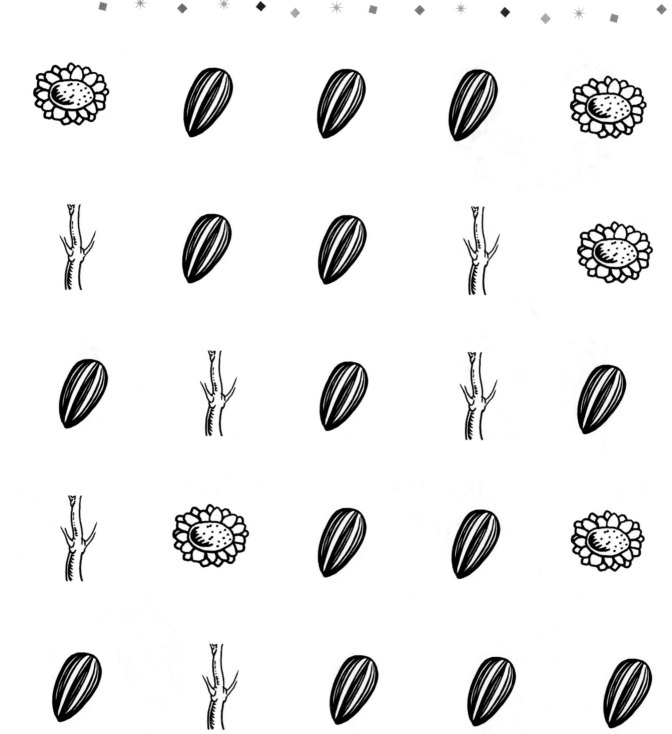

How many seeds did you circle? _____

Nombre: _____

flor   sistema
              de raíces

planta   tallo

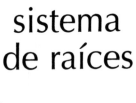

flor   sistema
              de raíces

semilla   hoja

hoja   planta

semilla   flor

Name: _____

 **Plant Part Circle**   Circle the correct name of each plant part.

flower   root system

plant   stem

flower   root system

seed   leaf

leaf   plant

seed   flower

Nombre: _____

 Deletrea las partes de la planta

_____ _____ _____

_____ _____ _____

Name: _____

 Plant Part Spell

_____ | _____ | _____

_____ | _____ | _____

Nombre: _____

 Cuenta las partes de la planta.

¿Cuántas semillas? _____

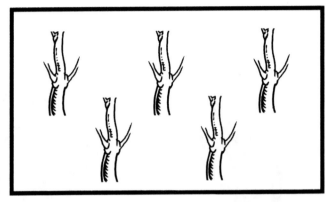

¿Cuántos tallos? _____

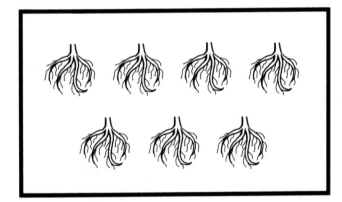

¿Cuántos sistemas de raíces? _____

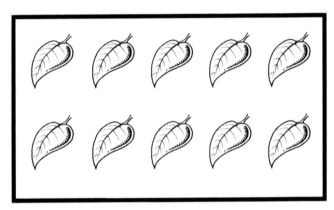

¿Cuántas hojas? _____

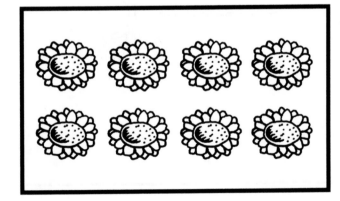

¿Cuántas flores? _____

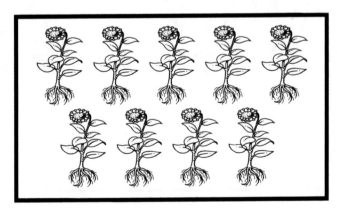

¿Cuántas plantas? _____

Name: _____

 Count the plant parts.

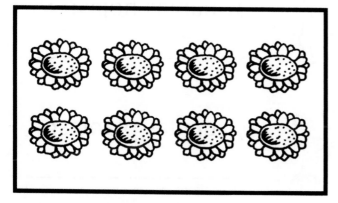

How many seeds? _____

How many stems? _____

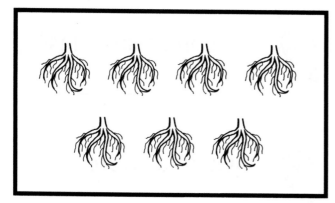

How many root systems?

_____

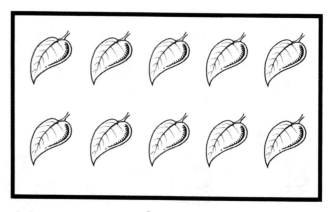

How many leaves? _____

How many flowers? _____

How many plants? _____

Nombre: _____

 Cuenta las partes de la planta. Escribe el número en letras.

   ¿Cuántos sistemas de raíces?

_____

    ¿Cuántos tallos?

_____

     ¿Cuántas semillas?

_____

     ¿Cuántas flores?

_____

     ¿Cuántas hojas?

_____

      ¿Cuántas plantas?

_____

Name: _____

 Plant Part Count   *Write the number word.*

       How many root systems?

_____

       How many stems?

_____

       How many seeds?

_____

       How many flowers?

_____

       How many leaves?

_____

      How many plants?

_____

Nombre: _____

Problemas de matemáticas

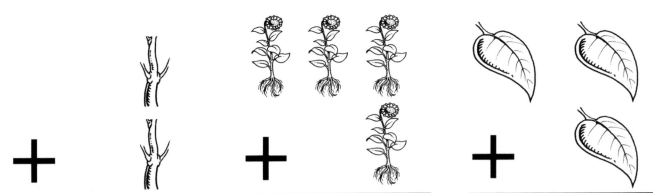

$$+ \qquad \qquad +$$

$$+ \qquad \qquad + \qquad \qquad +$$

$$+ \quad = \quad \underline{\hspace{2cm}}$$

$$+ \quad = \quad \underline{\hspace{2cm}}$$

$$+ \quad = \quad \underline{\hspace{2cm}}$$

Plant Part Addition

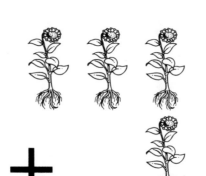 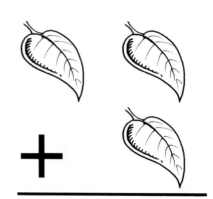

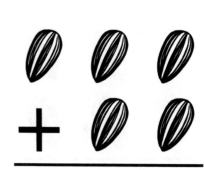

Problemas de matemáticas

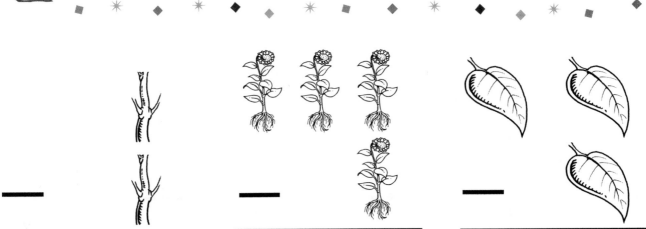

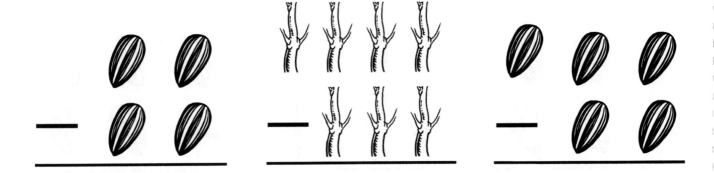

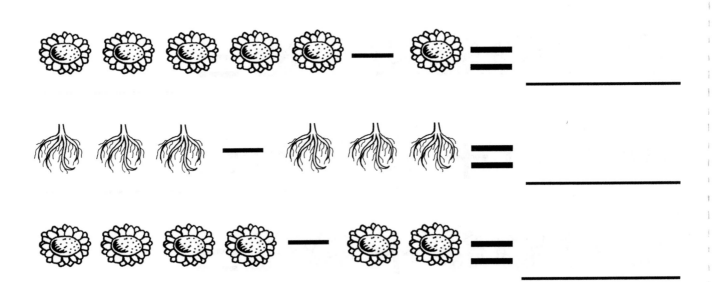

Name: _____

▣ Plant Part Subtraction

   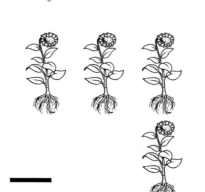   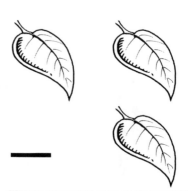

____

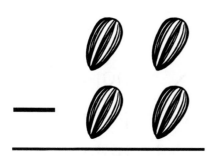   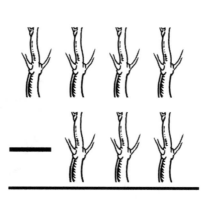   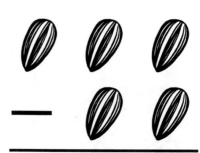

 =

_____

 =

_____

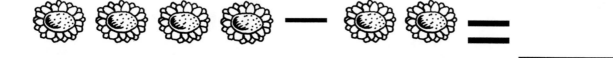 =

_____

Nombre: _____

   sistema de raíces
sistem del raíces
sistema de raizes

   semila
semilla
semmila

   flar
flor
floar

   hoja
joha
hojo

   plan
planto
planta

   tallo
thallo
talo

© Carson-Dellosa • Plantas • Plants • FI-704015

Name: _____

 **Spell It Correctly**   Circle the word that is spelled correctly in each group.

   root system
rute system
root sistem

   sead
seed
ceed

   flour
flower
fluor

   leaf
leef
laef

   plante
plan
plant

   stem
stemn
stam

Nombre: _____

 **Llena los espacios** Escribe la letra que falta en cada palabra.

__lanta

__emilla

__oja

__lor

__istema de raíces

__allo

Fill in the Blanks   Fill in the missing letter in each word.

__lant

__eed

__eaf

__lower

__oot system

__tem

Nombre: _____

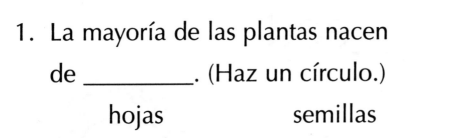

Las plantas son seres vivos. La mayoría de las plantas nacen de semillas. Las plantas tienen raíces, tallos y hojas. Algunas plantas tienen flores. Algunas plantas viven adentro y otras viven afuera.

1. La mayoría de las plantas nacen

   de _____. (Haz un círculo.)

   hojas   semillas

2. Las plantas son seres vivos. (Haz un círculo.)

   cierto   falso

3. Todas las plantas viven afuera. (Haz un círculo.)

   cierto   falso

4. Las plantas tienen raíces, tallos y _____.

   (Haz un círculo.)   hojas   hierba

BONO:

- ¿Cuántos verbos hay en el párrafo anterior? _____

- Haz un círculo alrededor de la segunda palabra en cada oración.

- Subraya cada sustantivo en el párrafo anterior.

Name: _____

 **Plants**   Read the paragraph. Answer the questions. Color the picture.

Plants are living things. Most plants come from seeds. Plants have roots, stems, and leaves. Some plants have flowers. Some plants live indoors, and others live outside.

1. Most plants come from _____.

    (Circle one.)   leaves   seeds

2. Plants are _____ things.

    (Circle one.)   dead   living

3. All plants live outside. (Circle one.)

                     true   false

4. Plants have roots, stems, and _____. (Circle one.)

                    leaves   grass

BONUS:

• How many verbs are in the paragraph above? _____

• Circle the second word in each sentence.

• Underline each noun in the paragraph above.

Nombre: _____

Lee el párrafo. Responde a las preguntas.

Una semilla contiene el principio de una planta nueva. La mayoría de las plantas nacen de las semillas. Todas las semillas se convierten en el mismo tipo de planta que produjo la semilla. Las semillas viajan a través del viento, el aire y el agua. Cuando la semilla encuentra un poco de tierra, sol y agua, germina. Entonces la planta pequeña dentro de la semilla empieza a crecer.

1. Las semillas contienen el principio de una planta nueva.

   (Haz un círculo.)   cierto   falso

2. Las semillas pueden viajar a través del aire.

   (Haz un círculo.)   sí   no

3. La mayoría de las plantas nacen de _____.

   (Haz un círculo.)   huevos   semillas

4. Cuando encuentra la tierra, el sol y el agua, la semilla _____.

   (Haz un círculo.)   se cae   germina

5. Todas las semillas se convierten en el mismo tipo de planta que la produjo.

   (Haz un círculo.)   cierto   falso

Name: _____

 **Seeds**

A seed contains the beginnings of a new plant. Most plants come from seeds. All seeds grow into the same kinds of plants that made the seeds. Seeds can travel by wind, air, and water. When the seed lands on a bit of soil and is given sun and water, it germinates. That means the baby plant inside the seed starts to grow.

1. Seeds have the beginnings of a new plant inside.

    (Circle one.)   true   false

2. Seeds can travel by air.

    (Circle one.)   yes   no

3. Most plants come from _____.

    (Circle one.)   eggs   seeds

4. When the seed finds soil, sun, and water, it _____.

    (Circle one.)   falls   germinates

5. All seeds grow into the same kinds of plants that made the seeds.

    (Circle one.)   true   false

Nombre: _____

 **Los tallos**   Lee el párrafo. Responde a las preguntas. Colorea el dibujo.

Los tallos llevan el agua y los minerales desde las raíces hasta las hojas. Los tallos también pueden ayudar a las plantas a enderezarse y a tomar el sol. El tallo de un árbol se llama un tronco. La mayoría de los tallos crecen hacia arriba.

1. Los tallos llevan agua a las hojas.

   (Haz un círculo.)   cierto   falso

2. Los tallos ayudan a las plantas a enderezarse.

   (Haz un círculo.)   cierto   falso

3. El tallo de un árbol se llama un tronco.

   (Haz un círculo.)   cierto   falso

4. La mayoría de los tallos crecen _____.

   (Haz un círculo)   hacia arriba   en la tierra

BONO:

- Haz un círculo alrededor de cada punto en el párrafo anterior.

- ¿Cuántas veces puedes encontrar la palabra "los" en el párrafo anterior? _____

   © Carson-Dellosa • Plantas • Plants • FI-704015

Name: _____

 **Stems**   Read the paragraph. Answer the questions. Color the picture.

Stems carry water and minerals from the roots of a plant to its leaves. Stems can also help a plant stand upright and receive sunlight. The stem of a tree is called a trunk. Most stems grow upward.

1. Stems carry water to the leaves.

    (Circle one.)   true   false

2. Stems help a plant stand up straight.

    (Circle one.)   true   false

3. The stem of a tree is called a trunk.

    (Circle one.)   true   false

4. Most stems grow _____.

    (Circle one.)   upward   on the ground

BONUS:

*   Circle each period in the paragraph above.

*   How many times is the word "and" used in the paragraph above? _____

Nombre: _____

 **El sistema de raíces**

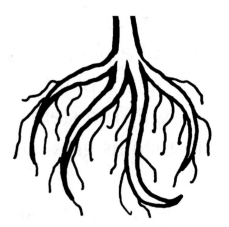

Las raíces ayudan a alimentar a la planta obteniendo el agua y los minerales de la tierra. Las raíces también ayudan a fijar la planta a la tierra. Ejemplos de raíces que comemos son las zanahorias y remolachas.

1. Las raíces ayudan a alimentar a las plantas.

   (Haz un círculo.)   cierto   falso

2. Las raíces ayudan a fijar la planta a _____.

   (Haz un círculo.)   la tierra   el aire

3. Un ejemplo de las raíces que se comen son _____.

   (Haz un círculo.)   las zanahorias y remolachas

                          las naranjas y las manzanas

BONO:

- ¿Cuántos sustantivos hay en el párrafo anterior? _____

- Subraya la penúltima palabra de cada oración del párrafo anterior.

Name: _____

 **Root Systems**   Read the paragraph. Answer the questions. Color the picture.

Roots help feed a plant by getting water and minerals from the soil. The roots also help hold the plant in the ground. Some roots are good to eat, like carrots and beets.

1. Roots help feed the plant.

    (Circle one.)   true   false

2. Roots help hold the plant in the _____.

    (Circle one.)   ground   air

3. Examples of roots that people eat are _____.

    (Circle one.)   carrots and beets

                          oranges and apples

BONUS:

• How many nouns are in the paragraph above? _____

• Underline the second to last word in each sentence in the paragraph above.

Nombre: _____

 **Las hojas**   Lee el párrafo. Responde a las preguntas. Colorea el dibujo.

    Las hojas producen la mayoría del alimento que necesita una planta para vivir y crecer. Las plantas usan sus hojas verdes, el agua de la tierra y el sol para producir su propio alimento. Las hojas pueden ser de tamaños y formas diferentes. Algunas plantas tienen una hoja en cada tallo. Otras plantas tienen más de una hoja por tallo.

1. Las hojas producen la mayoría del alimento que necesita la planta.

    (Haz un círculo.)   cierto   falso

2. Las plantas usan el agua, sus hojas y el sol para producir su alimento.

    (Haz un círculo)   cierto   falso

3. Las hojas son de tamaños y _____ diferentes.

    (Haz un círculo)   colores   formas

4. Todas las plantas tienen cuatro hojas por tallo.

    (Haz un círculo)   cierto   falso

BONO:

- ¿Cuántas veces encuentras la palabra "la" en el párrafo anterior? _____

Name: _____

 **Leaves**   Read the paragraph. Answer the questions. Color the picture.

Leaves make most of the food a plant needs to live and grow. Plants use their green leaves, water from the ground, air, and sunlight to make their own food. Leaves can be many different shapes and sizes. Some plants grow one leaf on each stem. Other plants grow more than one leaf on one stem.

1. Leaves make most of the food a plant needs.

   (Circle one.)   true   false

2. Plants use water, their leaves, and sunlight to make food.

   (Circle one.)   true ·   false

3. Leaves are many different _____ and sizes.

   (Circle one.)   stems   shapes

4. All plants grow four leaves on each stem.

   (Circle one.)   true   false

BONUS:

- How many times is the word "to" used in the paragraph above? _____

Nombre: _____

 **Las flores**   Lee el párrafo. Responde a las preguntas. Colorea el dibujo.

Las flores son de formas, tamaños y colores diferentes. Las flores producen semillas. Una flor tiene muchas partes. Las flores atraen a las abejas y otros insectos.

1. Las flores son solamente de una forma.

   (Haz un círculo.)   cierto   falso

2. Las flores producen _____.

   (Haz un círculo.)   tallos   semillas

3. La flor tiene _____ parte.

   (Haz un círculo.)   solamente una   más de una

4. A las abejas les gustan _____.

   (Haz un círculo.)   las flores   los tallos

BONO:

• ¿Cuántos sustantivos encuentras en el párrafo anterior?

   _____

• ¿Cuántas veces se ha usado la letra "f" como la primera letra de una palabra en el párrafo anterior? _____

Name: _____

 **Flowers**   Read the paragraph. Answer the questions. Color the picture.

   Flowers come in many shapes, sizes, and colors. Flowers produce seeds. A flower is made up of many parts. Flowers attract bees and other insects.

1. Flowers come in only one shape.

    (Circle one.)   true   false

2. Flowers produce _____.

    (Circle one.)   stems   seeds

3. A flower has _____ part.

    (Circle one.)   only one   more than one

4. Bees like _____.

    (Circle one.)   flowers   stems

BONUS:

• How many nouns are in the paragraph above? _____

• How many times is the letter "f" used as the first letter in a word in the paragraph above? _____

Answer Key

Page 44
1. hoja, 2. flor, 3. tallo,
4. semilla, 5. sistema de raíces

Page 45
1. leaf, 2. flower, 3. stem,
4. seed, 5. root system

Page 46

Page 47

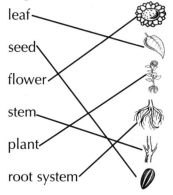

Pages 48–49
6 hojas/leaves

Pages 50–51
14 semillas/seeds

Page 52
From left to right and top to bottom: flor, tallo, sistema de raíces, hoja, planta, semilla

Page 53
From left to right and top to bottom: flower, stem, root system, leaf, plant, seed

Page 54
From left to right and top to bottom: semilla, flor, hoja, sistema de raíces, tallo, planta

Page 55
From left to right and top to bottom: seed, flower, leaf, root system, stem, plant

Pages 56–57
From left to right and top to bottom: 6, 5, 7, 10, 8, 9

Page 58
dos, uno, tres, cuatro, dos, tres

Page 59
two, one, three, four, two, three

Pages 60–61
From left to right and top to bottom: 2, 4, 3, 4, 7, 5, 6, 6, 6

Pages 62–63
From left to right and top to bottom: 0, 2, 1, 0, 1, 1, 4, 0, 2

Page 64
From left to right and top to bottom: sistema de raíces, semilla, flor, hoja, planta, tallo

Page 65
From left to right and top to bottom: root system, seed, flower, leaf, plant, stem

Page 66
planta, semilla, hoja, flor, sistema de raíces, tallo

Page 67
plant, seed, leaf, flower, root system, stem

Page 68
1. semillas, 2. cierto, 3. falso,
4. hojas, BONO: 6 verbos;
plantas, mayoría, plantas, plantas,
and *plantas* should be circled;
plantas, seres, plantas, semillas,
plantas, raíces, tallos, hojas,
plantas, flores, and *plantas* should
be underlined.

Page 69
1. seeds, 2. living, 3. false,
4. leaves, BONUS: 6 verbs; *are,*
plants, have, plants, and *plants*
should be circled; *Plants, things,*
plants, seeds, Plants, roots, stems,
leaves, plants, flowers, and *plants*
should be underlined.

Page 70
1. cierto, 2. sí, 3. semillas,
4. germina, 5. cierto

Page 71
1. true, 2. yes, 3. seeds,
4. germinates, 5. true

Page 72
1. cierto, 2. cierto, 3. cierto, 4. hacia
arriba, BONO: 4 periods; 4

Page 73
1. true, 2. true, 3. true, 4. upward,
BONUS: 4 periods; 2

Page 74
1. cierto, 2. la tierra, 3. las
zanahorias y remolachas,
BONO: 11; *la, la,* and *y* should
be underlined.

Page 75
1. true, 2. ground, 3. carrots and
beets, BONUS: 11; *the, the,* and
and should be underlined.

Page 76
1. cierto, 2. cierto, 3. formas,
4. falso, BONO: 2

Page 77
1. true, 2. true, 3. shapes, 4. false,
BONUS: 2

Page 78
1. falso, 2. semillas, 3. más de
una, 4. las flores, BONO: 11; 5

Page 79
1. false, 2. seeds, 3. more than
one, 4. flowers, BONUS: 11; 4